A Mom's Book of Encouragement

THIS BOOK BELONGS TO

Dena Dupeire

Loveland, Colorado | group.com

Group resources really work!

This Group resource incorporates our R.E.A.L. approach to ministry. It reinforces a growing friendship with Jesus, encourages long-term learning, and results in life transformation, because it's:

Relational—Learner-to-learner interaction enhances learning and builds Christian friendships.

Experiential—What learners experience through discussion and action sticks with them up to 9 times longer than what they simply hear or read.

Applicable—The aim of Christian education is to equip learners to be both hearers and doers of God's Word.

Learner-based—Learners understand and retain more when the learning process takes into consideration how they learn best.

A Mom's Book of Encouragement

Visit our website: **group.com/women**

This resource is brought to you by the wildly creative women's ministry team at Group. Choose Group resources for your women's ministry, and experience the difference! Additional moms who contributed to this book include:

Linda Crawford
Jenifer Jernigan
Cheryl Meakins
Amber Van Schooneveld
Jill Wuellner

Unless otherwise indicated, all Scripture quotations are taken from the *Holy Bible*, New Living Translation, copyright © 1996, 2004, 2007 by Tyndale House Foundation. Used by permission of Tyndale House Publishers, Inc., Carol Stream, Illinois 60188. All rights reserved.

ISBN 978-1-4707-0453-7

Printed in the United States of America.

10 9 8 7 6 5 4 3 2 1   22 21 20 19 18 17 16 15 14 13

···· Contents ····

Welcome
to
A Year of
ENCOURAGMENT!

This year as you join with other moms at Where Moms Connect, you'll find encouragement every time you're together—encouragement on the journey of momhood, encouragement to lift your heart, and encouragement in your relationship with God.

This book will be your guide every step of the way. Tucked in these pages are all the notes, Bible verses, reflections, and other content you'll need to participate each time you gather at Where Moms Connect. Be sure to bring this book along when you meet.

We know that as a mom you're busy. But we also know you care about growing yourself spiritually, emotionally, and mentally. So along with the content for each session of Where Moms Connect, we've included additional notes for you to read and reflect on if you have time. Sometimes it's a devotion, sometimes a few verses or lyrics to a song, other times just a short thought to reflect on. These are for you to use as you want, as you have time, with no guilt and no pressure.

Thanks for joining other moms at Where Moms Connect. We hope this truly is a year of encouragement for you on your journey in momhood.

The Courage to Encourage

Connecting to the Topic

What affects our ability to encourage?

• Thinking we have to give answers.

• Thinking we have none of the answers.

Connecting With God

The Bible talks about encouragement in many places. Here are just a few verses to consider; take turns reading these aloud in your group.

"Dear brothers and sisters, I close my letter with these last words: Be joyful. Grow to maturity. Encourage each other. Live in harmony and peace. Then the God of love and peace will be with you." (2 Corinthians 13:11)

"When we get together, I want to encourage you in your faith, but I also want to be encouraged by yours." (Romans 1:12)

"Don't use foul or abusive language. Let everything you say be good and helpful, so that your words will be an encouragement to those who hear them." (Ephesians 4:29)

"So encourage each other and build each other up, just as you are already doing." (1 Thessalonians 5:11)

Heb. 10:25

Discuss with your group:

- Which of these verses sort of "jumps out" to you, and why?

- Why do you think encouraging one another is such an important part of living the life God desires for us?

- How can these verses help you grow in putting the "en" (the action) into *encourage*—both in giving and receiving encouragement?

Connecting to My Life

_____

_____

_____

_____

_____

_____

_____

_____

_____

_____

_____

_____

_____

_____

_____

_____

_____

_____

_____

_____

Additional Thoughts on Encouragement

This week reread the verses from this session. Read them as often as you like, thinking about how these words touch your heart.

Think about the people who have encouraged you in the past few weeks. Write their names below. Perhaps you'd like to write a note or e-mail of thanks to one of them. Even if you don't have time for that, thank God for the people of encouragement he has put in your life, and ask God to help you have more courage to encourage others!

_____

_____

_____

_____

_____

_____

_____

_____

_____

_____

_____

_____

_____

_____

Lighten Up!
De-stress, and Lift Your Spirits

Connecting to the Topic

- How do you deal with stress in your life?

- What have you found that's helpful?

Connecting With God

Six Ways to Turn Down the Stress in Your Life

1. **Simplify.** Appointments, tasks, meetings, commitments… trimming the list reduces stress and opens up room to imagine, play, and enjoy life. You can't do it all, so do what matters most.

2. **Live in the present.** Worried about tomorrow? Replaying what happened yesterday? Today is what you have. Today is what you can impact. Give attention to today.

"So don't worry about tomorrow, for tomorrow will bring its own worries. Today's trouble is enough for today." (Matthew 6:34)

3. **Visit your "happy place."** Calming mental vacations are as easy as recalling that trip to the beach or hike through the mountains. Close your eyes, and recall every detail—the sights, sounds, and smells. Let the warm relaxation wash across you.

4. Treat yourself well. You're a mom—you know this stuff! Eat healthy foods. Drink enough water. Get needed sleep. Exercise. Care for your body, and it will sustain you. And forgive yourself—you're only human.

"In peace I will lie down and sleep, for you alone, O Lord, will keep me safe." (Psalm 4:8)

5. Think positively. Be intentional about filling your life with what's uplifting. What you feed, grows—including cynicism and stress. So feed humor and joy.

"Fix your thoughts on what is true, and honorable, and right, and pure, and lovely, and admirable. Think about things that are excellent and worthy of praise." (Philippians 4:8)

6. Share the load. With family, with God, with friends at Where Moms Connect—share what's troubling you. Let others know you're stressed, and be open to receiving their care and concern.

"Don't worry about anything; instead, pray about everything. Tell God what you need, and thank him for all he has done. Then you will experience God's peace, which exceeds anything we can understand. His peace will guard your hearts and minds as you live in Christ Jesus." (Philippians 4:6-7)

Connecting to My Life

_____

_____

_____

_____

_____

_____

_____

_____

_____

_____

_____

_____

_____

_____

_____

_____

_____

_____

_____

_____

Additional Thoughts on Lightening Up

Read through the "Six Ways to Turn Down the Stress in Your Life" again. Instead of saying "Oh, I can't do that!" to each one, take a couple minutes to consider what it might look like if you *did* do each one. Ideas that seem impossible at first might actually be doable.

Circle or highlight ideas you could give a try. After a few days, come back and jot down your notes. What worked? What could you try next?

_____

_____

_____

_____

_____

_____

_____

_____

_____

_____

_____

_____

_____

_____

_____

Praying for and With Your Children

Connecting to the Topic

Here's one idea for using the sense of touch in a time of prayer for yourself or with your family. Choose something that has an interesting texture—for example, a blanket, a stuffed animal, an emery board, or a rock. What do you like about this texture? What might this texture reflect about the nature of God? A soft blanket could reflect the comfort of God. A rough rock could remind us that God is with us in rough times. How could the texture of this item guide a prayer?

Here's an idea for using the sense of taste in a time of prayer for yourself or with your family. Sample several foods, really taking time to chew slowly and taste all the flavors of the food. Taste something bitter (like cocoa powder), and pray about something that is bitter in your life, such as a difficult relationship. Taste something sweet, and thank God for the sweet people in your life. Taste something spicy, and thank God for the people who spice up your life! This idea could easily be adapted to work with the sense of smell, as well.

- Brainstorm other ideas that could bring the senses of sight, hearing, touch, smell, and taste into a time of prayer. Write your thoughts here.

_____

_____

_____

Connecting With God

- How can the ideas we shared so far help prayer seem less intimidating for you or your children?

_____

_____

_____

_____

_____

A few moms in the group can read these verses aloud:

"Don't worry about anything; instead, pray about everything. Tell God what you need, and thank him for all he has done. Then you will experience God's peace, which exceeds anything we can understand. His peace will guard your hearts and minds as you live in Christ Jesus." (Philippians 4:6-7)

"Always be joyful. Never stop praying. Be thankful in all circumstances, for this is God's will for you who belong to Christ Jesus." (1 Thessalonians 5:16-18)

"The Lord is close to all who call on him, yes, to all who call on him in truth." (Psalm 145:18)

- How do these words give you confidence to pray for and with your children?

_____

_____

_____

_____

_____

Connecting to My Life

_____

_____

_____

_____

_____

_____

_____

_____

_____

_____

_____

_____

_____

_____

_____

_____

Additional Thoughts on Prayer

"I am praying to you because I know you will answer, O God. Bend down and listen as I pray." (Psalm 17:6)

Good morning! Pour yourself a cup of coffee, and pull up a chair so we can chat. In fact, why don't we begin with a word of prayer: *"Our most gracious heavenly Father, who knowest what we needst and supplieth it..."*

Okay, now that we have had a word of prayer, why don't we have a word *about* prayer? Why does the thought of talking to God intimidate us so much? Is it because we think we must sound so stiff and formal?

No doubt prayer is important to God. Jesus prayed consistently and taught his followers to do the same. He wants to hear from us in the same way! Yet, we fret too much over what to say and how to say it. If we speak, we want our words to sound like a work of art to God's ears. However, we get so busy agonizing over our would-be prayer life that we forget to actually pray. Today, let's freshen up our approach to conversation with God.

Think about your favorite friend. This friend knows the sound of your voice, your tone, the words you're likely to use, and the ones you never use. You know the same about her. You know each other inside and out. Guess what? God knows *you* inside and out. His desire is for you to know him intimately, as well. Jesus desires comfortable communication with you.

So forget the fancy lingo. Forget how someone else might address the Almighty. The Lord only wants you to talk to him like *you* would talk to him. Imagine yourself pulling up a chair and chatting with Jesus as your dearest friend. The more you chat, the dearer you become to each other.

Just remember one thing as you pray: God is leaning close to hear from you. To him, your words are a masterpiece.

What's on your mind right now that you'd like to share with God? Remember, just be yourself!

Does God Have a Plan

for You?

Connecting to My Life

My puzzle piece...and my reflections from my time of prayer.

_____

_____

_____

_____

_____

_____

_____

_____

_____

_____

_____

_____

_____

_____

Additional Thoughts on God's Plan for Me

Write thoughts here about the dreams you've had for your life and the ones you still have.

_____

_____

_____

_____

_____

_____

Think about what God's plans might be, what your plans might be, and how they overlap. Reflect on this verse: "We can make our plans, but the Lord determines our steps" (Proverbs 16:9). Ask God for direction on the steps for your life. Write your thoughts below.

_____

_____

_____

_____

_____

_____

Creating Balance

Connecting With God

- Share how you felt during the group juggling session. Was it fun or frustrating? Or did some other emotion spring to the surface?

- How are the feelings or attitudes you experienced while doing the group juggling similar to or different from the way you feel about juggling all the activities and responsibilities of your daily life?

One mom in the group can read these verses aloud:

"Then Jesus said, 'Come to me, all of you who are weary and carry heavy burdens, and I will give you rest. Take my yoke upon you. Let me teach you, because I am humble and gentle at heart, and you will find rest for your souls. For my yoke is easy to bear, and the burden I give you is light.'" (Matthew 11:28-30)

- What do you think the "yoke" Jesus mentions is all about?

As you're considering this, read Matthew 6:33, and see if that gives you any insights: "Seek the Kingdom of God above all else, and live righteously, and he will give you everything you need."

- How do these words from Jesus encourage you in the midst of trying to juggle or balance all your responsibilities and relationships?

Connecting to My Life

_____

_____

_____

_____

_____

_____

_____

_____

_____

_____

_____

_____

_____

_____

_____

_____

_____

_____

_____

A *Moms* Book of *Encouragement* ·····································

Additional Thoughts on Creating Balance

"Each time he said, 'My grace is all you need. My power works best in weakness.' So now I am glad to boast about my weaknesses, so that the power of Christ can work through me." (2 Corinthians 12:9)

"He gives power to the weak and strength to the powerless." (Isaiah 40:29)

God's power works best in our weakness. But what does that mean? Are we to act helpless, give up, and expect God to do all the work? What does powerlessness really look like?

Picture an 8-month-old baby sitting on your lap...but not for long. Soon she wants to stand and bounce up and down on her legs while you steady her to keep her from falling. Up and down, up and down, pushing those little legs to show you just how strong they are! Yet she can't walk. Sure, her legs are strong enough at 8 months, but something is missing. Without your strong, steadying presence, it would be impossible for her to stand, bounce up and down, or take a few steps.

She needs you. She needs you to be for her what she can't give herself right now—her core strength. Without you, her legs are powerless to hold her body up. But does she act helpless, give up, and wait for you to do all the work? No, she trusts you to do for her what she cannot do for herself and depends on your strength to help her risk trying things that are beyond her ability to achieve right now. In time, those weaknesses will become strengths, and she'll squeal with delight when she takes her first steps.

Why can't babies walk? Why can't you walk on a tightrope? dance like a ballerina? The answer is core body strength. Dynamic balance for any activity comes from strength in the center of our bodies. If you tip over easily when you stand on one foot, it's due mostly to poor core strength, not lack of strength in your legs.

Just like babies, we develop our weaknesses into strengths by starting from a position of weakness before God. We can't walk a balanced life without trusting in God as the source of our strength. Trusting not just with our minds, but with the very core of our being. Once we have developed a core of trust and reliance on God, we can start to move. But wait! Before we can stand, run, or jump, we must first *kneel* because prayer is our power position—it's where we get plugged in to God as our source of strength.

Dealing With
Loneliness

Connecting to the Topic

Here are four different ideas for dealing with loneliness. Take turns reading each one aloud, and then discuss the questions that follow with the other moms in your group.

1. **Spend time with people.** Maybe this seems obvious—but when we feel lonely we often shut down and stay away from people. Loneliness sometimes causes depression that cuts us off from people. When you're lonely, decide to reach out, no matter how you feel. Reconnect with an old friend. Join a social club or a church choir. Reestablish a relationship with God. Come to Where Moms Connect! Force yourself to be open to people—and seek them out.

2. **Pick up a hobby.** Restarting or learning a new hobby or skill is a great way to keep your mind active. As Tom Sutherland shared, mental activity is a key to keeping yourself from feeling lonely. An added benefit is that if you're in a pottery class, for instance, you'll be with people who enjoy something you enjoy, people with whom you can spend time as a mentor or a person being mentored.

3. **Volunteer.** Not only will you be in contact with people, but when you volunteer doing something you're good at, it builds self-esteem, too. Volunteer in roles that put you in contact with people you can help, with causes you care about. (Have you ever thought about volunteering with the Where Moms Connect team? ☺)

4. Get a pet. You might think this idea is only for older people—not for busy moms who don't need another creature to care for. But having a pet is a great way to begin recovering from loneliness, even for moms! Pick a pet that fits your activity and lifestyle, and it helps if it's a pet that will actually respond to you.

Discuss:

- Which of these four are you likeliest to do if you're lonely? Perhaps one of them is a strategy you've used in the past during lonely times. Share about that.

- Which of the other three steps would you be *least* likely to try? Tell why.

- What other ideas can you share with the moms in your group that have helped you in lonely times?
  (Be sure to jot down any ideas someone shares that you want to remember!)

_____

_____

_____

_____

_____

_____

_____

_____

_____

_____

Additional Thoughts
on Dealing With Loneliness

Our prayer today was taken from Psalm 27:7-10. Read it again, and reflect on God's message to you:

"Hear me as I pray, O Lord.

Be merciful and answer me!

My heart has heard you say, 'Come and talk with me.'

And my heart responds, 'Lord, I am coming.'

Do not turn your back on me.

Do not reject your servant in anger.

You have always been my helper.

Don't leave me now; don't abandon me,

O God of my salvation!

Even if my father and mother abandon me, the Lord will hold me close."

- Who was the person you thought of when you were asked about someone who desperately needs a friend? Is this someone you could reach out to? How? Is this someone you could be praying for? Get started!

_____

_____

_____

_____

_____

Notes

_____

_____

_____

_____

_____

_____

_____

_____

_____

_____

_____

_____

_____

_____

_____

_____

_____

Affordable Fun
for Families

Connecting to the Topic

Read through this list of ideas for affordable fun together. Take turns around the table reading each item.

- Write a story or a comic book together.

- Go on a vacation without leaving your house—go camping in the backyard on a nice summer night, toasted marshmallows and all.

- Depending on the time of year, build a gingerbread house, decorate valentine cookies, or make another holiday-themed treat.

- Create a scavenger hunt or treasure hunt around the house, with clues hidden in different places leading up to a prize.

- Have your children write and perform a play. You can help them with the script and come up with fun costumes from items around the house.

- Build paper airplanes, and have a flying contest.

- For the young ones in your family, create a couch fort or blanket fort. (Actually, a lot of teens like to do this too! ☺)

- In the winter, make ice-cream together out of snow.

- Get outside—ride a bike, take a hike, or throw a Frisbee at the park.

- Play hide-and-seek.

- Have a family talent show. Work with your kids to find fun performances to do.

- Create decorations for different holidays or seasons, and hang them around the house together.

- Volunteer at a charity together, such as helping out at a soup kitchen.

- Find easy science experiments to try at home.

- Three words: water balloon fight.

Now brainstorm some of your own ideas together.

_____

_____

_____

_____

Connecting With God

One woman can read this verse aloud to the table group: "The joy of the Lord is your strength" (Nehemiah 8:10).

- When do you most often feel joy?

- What do you think it means that the joy of the Lord is our strength?

- What do you think the joy of the Lord has to do with having fun with our families?

Have one mom read this verse: "[God] richly gives us all we need for our enjoyment" (1 Timothy 6:17).

- How do you think this verse relates to creating fun times with our families?

Connecting to My Life

Write a one- to two-sentence summary of your mission and purpose in creating fun and memorable times for your family. It might sound something like this:

"My mission is to create a fun and loving atmosphere that helps my children to grow up experiencing the joy of the Lord. I commit my family to God and ask that he would guide me in helping them rejoice in him."

This is just an idea—create your own mission statement!

My Mission for Fun

_____

_____

_____

_____

_____

_____

_____

_____

_____

_____

_____

_____

_____

Additional Thoughts on Fun

"The joy of the Lord is your strength." (Nehemiah 8:10)

- When was the last time *you* had fun? Was it with or without your kids? Take time to jot down a list of things you still love to do. Things that make you laugh. Things that fill you with joy. Circle one to do this week!

_____

_____

_____

_____

_____

_____

_____

_____

Financial Freedom

Connecting to the Topic

Tips for Better Money Management

1. **Use a budget.** Design a system that works for you. Maybe it's paper and pencil, envelopes, or an electronic system such as mint.com or QuickBooks.

   - Create a plan for your money.

   - Record your expenditures as you spend.

   - Analyze and adjust your budget at the end of each month.

2. **Use credit wisely.**
   - Use credit cards for planned, budgeted items.

   - Record your spending as you use your cards.

   - Pay your balance in full each month.

   - If you can't do the three steps above, don't use credit cards.

3. **Get out of debt.**
   - Commit to avoid getting any further in debt.

   - Fix and roll your payments.

   - Accelerate your payments.

Where Is Your Money Going?

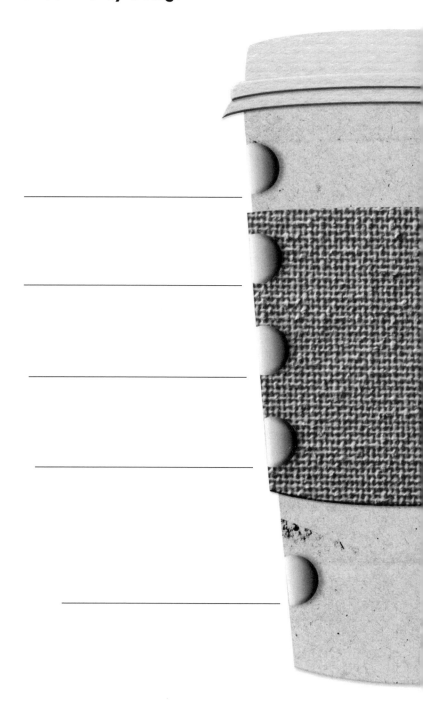

_____

_____

_____

_____

_____

Connecting With God

God's Plan

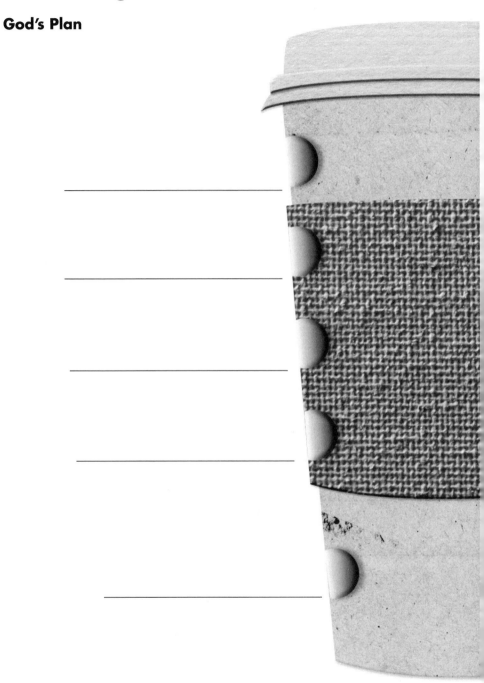

_____

_____

_____

_____

_____

Giving First

There are many places where the Bible talks about giving. Here are a few verses to consider:

"You must each decide in your heart how much to give. And don't give reluctantly or in response to pressure. 'For God loves a person who gives cheerfully.'" (2 Corinthians 9:7)

"Give generously to the poor, not grudgingly, for the Lord your God will bless you in everything you do." (Deuteronomy 15:10)

"All must give as they are able, according to the blessings given to them by the Lord your God." (Deuteronomy 16:17)

- Based on these and other verses you might know, what are your thoughts about making giving such a high priority in your budget?

_____

_____

_____

_____

_____

_____

- How can we, as moms, help our kids be cheerful and generous givers? What ideas can you share with the moms at your table?

_____

_____

_____

_____

Additional Thoughts on Giving

Sometimes remembering what others have given to us helps us as we think of giving. What have others given to get you where you are today? Think beyond money to other things such as time and effort.

- Jot down your thoughts here about what has been given to you.

_____

_____

_____

_____

The greatest gift that's been given to any of us is the gift of salvation that we have through Jesus. This cost more than we could ever imagine!

"For God loved the world so much that he gave his one and only Son, so that everyone who believes in him will not perish but have eternal life." (John 3:16)

- Write a note to God, sharing your thoughts on what he's given you through Jesus, through grace, through the promise of heaven, and more.

_____

_____

_____

_____

_____

_____

After you've written this note to God, reconsider what you have to give. Has your perspective changed? Something to think about. ☺

Notes

_____

_____

_____

_____

_____

_____

_____

_____

_____

_____

_____

_____

_____

_____

_____

_____

_____

Holiday Traditions

Connecting to the Topic

_____

_____

_____

_____

_____

_____

_____

_____

_____

_____

_____

_____

_____

_____

_____

_____

_____

_____

_____

_____

Holiday Fun

_____

_____

_____

_____

_____

_____

_____

_____

_____

_____

_____

_____

_____

_____

_____

_____

_____

_____

_____

_____

_____

Connecting With God

One mom in the group can read these verses aloud. Then discuss the questions that follow.

"We will use these stones to build a memorial. In the future your children will ask you, 'What do these stones mean?' Then you can tell them, 'They remind us that the Jordan River stopped flowing when the Ark of the Lord's Covenant went across.' These stones will stand as a memorial among the people of Israel forever." (Joshua 4:6-7)

- In what ways are holiday traditions like memorial stones? What do they help your children remember?

_____

_____

_____

_____

_____

_____

_____

_____

_____

_____

_____

_____

_____

_____

_____

"This annual festival will be a visible sign to you, like a mark branded on your hand or your forehead. Let it remind you always to recite this teaching of the Lord: 'With a strong hand, the Lord rescued you from Egypt.'" (Exodus 13:9)

- How can you use the following holidays to teach your children about God?

  Family Day
  Mother's Day
  Valentine's Day
  New Year's Day

_____

_____

_____

_____

_____

_____

_____

_____

_____

_____

_____

_____

_____

_____

_____

_____

Connecting to My Life

_____

_____

_____

_____

_____

_____

_____

_____

_____

_____

_____

_____

_____

_____

_____

_____

_____

Additional Thoughts on Traditions

Read this devotion whenever you have time.

"Search for the Lord and for his strength; continually seek him. Remember the wonders he has performed, his miracles, and the rulings he has given." (1 Chronicles 16:11-12)

We always seem to be looking ahead. From wondering what we'll be when we grow up to wondering when we'll retire, a good part of our days are spent looking forward. But one thing that's notable in the Old Testament, the Israelites always seemed to be looking backward. Moses encouraged the Israelites over and over to remember the miracles God had performed. They would set up monument after monument as reminders of where they had been. In his psalms, David often reminded himself of God's past kindness. God even gave the rainbow to serve as reminder of his mercy.

People always tell us not to dwell on the past, but clearly there must be *something* to this backward vision. For the Israelites, a good, solid reminder of what God had already done gave them faith to keep on following him. When hope seemed futile for David, memories of God's past mercies were the balm to his soul that revived him.

Memories are powerful things. Perhaps they are one of God's greatest gifts and teaching tools—and he provides us with them daily! They can correct negative thinking (*"Nothing good ever happens to me...oh wait, what about that one time..."*), bolster our faith (*"Well, God did come through last time..."*), or even just bring a smile to our faces (*"Remember that one time in Santa Fe...?"*).

C.S. Lewis wrote: "[A] pleasure is full grown only when it is remembered...What you call remembering is the last part of the pleasure." When we forget to remember all God's great blessings, we're missing a key part of the experience! Only in remembering them can we fully perceive their importance and beauty.

How can traditions you set in place for your family remind you to look back and remember what God has done?

The Bible

Connecting Together

What I saw...

_____

_____

_____

_____

Eugene Peterson quotes:

- "People knew the Bible really well, but all they wanted to do was study it, figure it out, and ask questions about it. And after a few years of that, I thought, 'They're not living any differently.'"

- "There's a lot of ambiguity in the Bible. There are a lot of answers you don't get. Don't insist on the Bible giving you answers."

- "The Bible does draw us into a holy community with both good and bad people. They're not separated out, but it's a holy community...It's a textbook for living in a community under God."

- "It's not the truth of the Bible that matters; it's the livability of the Bible."

Connecting to My Life

"All Scripture is inspired by God and is useful to teach us what is true and to make us realize what is wrong in our lives. It corrects us when we are wrong and teaches us to do what is right." (2 Timothy 3:16)

_____

_____

_____

_____

_____

_____

_____

_____

_____

_____

_____

_____

_____

_____

_____

Additional Thoughts on the Bible

Have you ever thought about the time you spend alone with God, reading the Bible, as a walk in a garden with him? Read the words to this hymn, and consider how spending time with God can be a peaceful walk with your best friend.

I Come to the Garden Alone

I come to the garden alone,
While the dew is still on the roses,
And the voice I hear falling on my ear
The Son of God discloses.
And he walks with me,
And he talks with me,
And he tells me I am his own;
And the joy we share as we tarry there,
None other has ever known.

He speaks, and the sound of his voice
Is so sweet the birds hush their singing;
And the melody that he gave to me
Within my heart is ringing.
And he walks with me,
And he talks with me,
And he tells me I am his own;
And the joy we share as we tarry there,
None other has ever known.

—Charles Austin Miles

Notes

_____
_____
_____
_____
_____
_____
_____
_____
_____
_____
_____
_____
_____
_____
_____
_____
_____
_____
_____
_____

Discipline for
All Ages

Connecting to the Topic

Opposing Plays

Review the scenario and the suggested coaching options. Decide which option your group prefers—or if you have different ideas entirely. Keep love in mind. ☺

Play 1: Dinnertime Dilemma

Ryan is 2 and almost "terrible"! He's the first child in his little family, so there are no brothers and sisters to watch him. Since learning to walk, Ryan has become very curious about his surroundings, pulling things off of shelves and out of cabinets, rearranging the coffee table décor every chance he gets, dumping the dog's food into her water dish, playing in the toilet water, and throwing tantrums when his mommy tells him no.

Anytime Ryan's mom turns her back, he becomes a magician, vanishing into thin air, sending her on a wild goose chase through the house looking for her curious toddler. Dinnertime seems to be the worst time of day for Ryan and his mom. Dinner always seems to burn, boil over in the oven, or not get cooked at all because Ryan's mom can't work in the kitchen for having to keep such a close eye on him.

What can mom do with him during dinnertime prep and cooking to ensure Ryan's safety and whereabouts while preparing her family's nightly meal?

Discuss these options, and decide which ones are good ideas, which are bad ideas, and see if you can think of any others to suggest:

- Spank him and put him in his bed until it's time to eat.

- Make a "Ryan cabinet" full of wooden spoons, bowls, and play food so that he can "prepare" dinner with her.

- Put Ryan in his high chair with a coloring sheet and crayons or a few of his cars and trucks, and allow him to have movie time while she prepares dinner.

- Other ideas:

_____

_____

_____

_____

_____

_____

_____

_____

_____

_____

_____

_____

_____

Play 2: The Princess Predicament

Chloe is 5 and is the baby in the family, with an older sister and brother. She's a free spirit, fluttering her way through each day sprinkled in her very own blend of "fairy dust." She is talkative and fearless and never meets a stranger. Chloe loves to have her nails painted and her hair fixed just so.

But Chloe and her momma have a few issues with her wardrobe. Chloe's mind thinks of princess skirts, dress-up high heels, it-doesn't-have-to-match kind of clothes. Her momma, on the other hand, thinks of practical, functional, what's-the-weather-going-to-be-like kind of clothes. Getting Chloe ready for school has become a battle, leaving both mom and Chloe frustrated, flustered, and late for work and school.

What could Chloe's mom do to make their mornings run more smoothly, getting Chloe dressed appropriately and everyone out the door on time? Discuss these options, and decide which ones are good ideas, which are bad ideas, and see if you can think of any others to suggest:

• Have a special shopping day in Chloe's closet, designing outfits that meet both mom's and daughter's approval, and then perform a fashion show for the rest of the family. With Chloe's help, hang these outfits in her closet, labeling them "Monday," "Tuesday," "Wednesday," "Thursday," and "Friday" so each morning she knows what she'll wear that day.

• Designate a trunk for all of Chloe's princess, fairy, dance, and other dress-up clothes, and set trunk hours when Chloe can dress any way she wants.

• Scream, yell, and threaten the loss of computer time if she doesn't wear what momma has picked out.

• Other ideas:

_____

_____

_____

_____

_____

_____

_____

_____

Play 3: The Pond Problem

Hiro turned 10 last month. From birth, his mom knew he'd be much different from his older sister, and she was right. He stuck his finger in the light socket for a terrible shock at 9 months, ate dog food at 18 months, and figured out how to unbuckle his seatbelt at 2. At 4, he began jumping down flights of stairs because he believed himself to be Batman. Rocks, sticks, dirt, and danger are his best friends.

Hiro is adventurous and fearless. His latest adventure had him guiding the neighborhood kids to the pond to scout out beavers. While there, Hiro got his foot stuck in the mud and left his school shoe a few feet under. When asked about the missing shoe, Hiro made up a tale, trying to save his behind because he knows the rules about going to the pond without adult supervision.

Hiro blatantly disobeyed, and he lied about what really happened at the pond. What should his mom do? Discuss these options, and decide which ones are good ideas, which are bad ideas, and see if you can think of any others to suggest:

- Have Hiro go down to the pond and search for the shoe, but even if he finds the shoe, have him, with his own money, buy a new pair of shoes.

- Go with Hiro to his friends' homes to apologize to those parents for taking these kids to the pond without an adult.

- Sit down with Hiro and talk with him, lovingly yet firmly, about what could have happened at the pond had the boys not been able to free him from the mud.

- Put Hiro on video games restriction for two weeks—one week for disobeying and one week for lying.

- Other ideas:

_____

_____

_____

_____

_____

_____

_____

_____

_____

_____

_____

_____

_____

_____

Play 4: Teenager Trials

Jacinta, 13, is beginning to come into her own, learning who she is and gaining more freedoms and responsibilities. These in-between years from childhood play to teen independence are trying and confusing for her and her mom. The mood swings, the changing body, and the teen drama keep everyone on their toes.

Compliant, soft-spoken, mild-mannered, obey-right-away Jacinta is now pushing against the authority in her life, questioning why and balking at instruction. Jacinta believes she has a right to do things her way, keeping a messy room, staying up past her bedtime, and deciding for herself when she'll obey her parents. Her mom does want to give Jacinta room to spread her wings and begin to fly solo, making decisions for herself, but her mom also knows that Jacinta must respect the authority figures in her life and live under the rules of her home.

What can Jacinta's mom do to give her daughter the room she needs to spread her wings and fly, yet continue to instill in her that she must honor and respect those in authority over her life and abide by the rules that have been set in place? Discuss these options, and decide which ones are good ideas, which are bad ideas, and see if you can think of any others to suggest:

- Lock Jacinta in her room until she's 35, sliding food trays under the door three times a day.

- Schedule a girls' night out. Go to a favorite shop, bookstore, restaurant, yogurt shop, or coffee house.
  Talk openly.

- Because Jacinta is testing the boundaries of following rules, maybe it's time to adjust some of the family rules. Together over hot chocolate, review the family rules, chore responsibilities, and freedoms. Listen openly to each other, and compromise where compromise is appropriate.

• Other ideas:

_____

_____

_____

_____

_____

_____

_____

_____

_____

_____

_____

_____

_____

_____

_____

_____

_____

_____

_____

_____

Creating a Plan

Setting boundaries—Our kids will repeatedly try to push our discipline game plan outside the boundaries we've set. We need to hold firm in where we've placed each of our parenting boundaries. Our children, whether they like it, understand it, or want it, need boundaries in their lives. Where there are boundaries, there's safety. Where there are boundaries, there's a level of control. Where there are boundaries, children grow and flourish.

• What are boundaries you've set for your kids?

_____

_____

_____

_____

_____

_____

• What tips can you share for enforcing those boundaries?

_____

_____

_____

_____

_____

_____

_____

Keeping tempers under control—Tempers can flare, both ours and our kids'. When we "lose it" and resort to screaming, it leaves our kids afraid, frustrated, and down on themselves—and it doesn't model a good solution for them to follow. When they lose their tempers, we have to have a game plan in place, as it's often hard to think of what to do in the midst of a tantrum.

- How do you keep your own temper in check when you're frustrated with your kids?

_____

_____

_____

_____

_____

_____

- What ideas have worked for you when your kids have had temper tantrums?

_____

_____

_____

_____

_____

_____

Adjusting expectations—At times we may place unrealistic expectations on our kids for their behavior. For example, a preschooler really can't sit still and be quiet for an hour—they're wired to wiggle. When we make demands of our children that are out of their realistic reach, we're setting them up for failure and frustration.

- Are any of your expectations of your kids potentially unrealistic? If so, how could you adapt those?

_____

_____

_____

_____

_____

_____

_____

_____

_____

_____

_____

_____

_____

_____

_____

Connecting to My Life

_____

_____

_____

_____

_____

_____

_____

_____

_____

_____

_____

_____

_____

_____

_____

_____

_____

_____

Additional Thoughts on Discipline

As you look to the Bible for encouragement on this topic, here are verses you can use to guide your own actions—and some you can help your children learn and apply, as well.

"Do not provoke your children to anger by the way you treat them. Rather, bring them up with the discipline and instruction that comes from the Lord." (Ephesians 6:4)

"A gentle answer deflects anger, but harsh words make tempers flare." (Proverbs 15:1)

"See that no one pays back evil for evil, but always try to do good to each other and to all people." (1 Thessalonians 5:15)

"Don't use foul or abusive language. Let everything you say be good and helpful, so that your words will be an encouragement to those who hear them." (Ephesians 4:29)

"Instead, be kind to each other, tenderhearted, forgiving one another, just as God through Christ has forgiven you." (Ephesians 4:32)

Are there others you'd like to remember? Jot them down here.

_____

_____

_____

_____

_____

_____

_____

Overcoming Hardship

Connecting Together

My notes and reflections:

_____

_____

_____

_____

_____

_____

_____

_____

_____

_____

_____

_____

_____

"God is our refuge and strength, always ready to help in times of trouble." (Psalm 46)

Additional Thoughts
on Overcoming Hardship

Read this devotion whenever you have time. ☺

"So be strong and courageous! Do not be afraid and do not panic before them. For the Lord your God will personally go ahead of you. He will neither fail you nor abandon you." (Deuteronomy 31:6)

Sometimes it's hard to think of what bravery has to do with everyday, modern life. We're not fighting any Philistines or dodging between walls of the Red Sea. Sure, the Israelites needed bravery, but what place does bravery really have in all the humdrum events that make up most of *our* existence? What does it have to do with the hardships of our lives today?

The virtue of bravery and the necessity for it didn't die with the Philistines. Even when we're just getting through the struggles of day-to-day life, bravery is what God commands from us. But perhaps the difference between the old days and now is that our bravery isn't necessarily shown through darting off on daring quests. Perhaps it's of more of a quiet nature.

The oak tree has long been a symbol of bravery: strong, immovable, and enduring. The oak doesn't bow to the winds; it isn't shaken by the storms. Bravery can be an attitude of strong immovability rather than an action. Think of all the little things in which you need to have an attitude of bravery: when your gas bill for the month is doubled; when your child is 30 minutes late getting home and you start to panic; when you don't know how to tell your supervisor there's no way you can make your deadline. Bravery is the attitude of trusting God to get you through each little event rather than panicking or despairing. God wants us to be unmoved in our faith that he will take care of us, just as he took care of the Israelites.

And he doesn't ask us to go it alone: "For the Lord your God will personally go ahead of you. He will neither fail you nor abandon you." We can face the trials of everyday life with bravery because we know God is with us, he is good, and he has good plans for us. We can be strong and immovable like the oak because we have an incredible God to trust.

Help Me
Get Organized!

Connecting to the Topic

Read through the list that corresponds to your table's topic; then take some time to share and brainstorm some of your own ideas.

Cooking/Meal Planning

- Set aside a time each week to do your meal planning and shopping. For example, plan to spend 30 minutes each Saturday morning to write out your meals for that week and make a grocery list.

- Keep a list of go-to meals you know your family likes and are easy to make. Rotate through this list so you aren't at a loss for what to make each week, but also have some variety.

- Once a week, have an easy dish such as "Breakfast for Dinner" to have one meal planned and taken care of. Come up with other ideas that suit your fancy, like "Saturday Night Frozen Pizza" or "Mac and Cheese Mondays." This can take the stress out of coming up with a different meal for each day of the week.

- When you prepare a meal, make more than you need, and freeze half of it. If you have a smaller family, freeze the meals in smaller portions so you can pull out one meal at a time when you're in a hurry.

- Keep a grocery list in an easy-to-find spot so as you run out of items, you (and your family members) can add them to the list rather than making lots of trips to the store.

- If cooking is not your cup of tea, find some easy alternatives for your family, such as a catering company that offers prepared meals, a warehouse store such as Costco that offers prepared meals, or a business that allows you to prepare meals at their premises to be frozen at home.

- Other great ideas:

- Clean room of clothes
- Say nothing negative or hurtful
- say only what is nice
- don't loose temper
- play w/ my kids

Cleaning

- Plan to tackle one cleaning task each day so the work doesn't become overwhelming. For example, you could do laundry on Wednesdays, dust on Thursdays, and vacuum on Fridays.

- Don't do it alone—get the family involved, depending on their ages. Have games, contests, or prizes for different cleaning tasks. For example, set a timer for 15 minutes for your children to clean their rooms. The first one who is done and on the couch wins.

- Assign family members different tasks as their responsibility. For example, if you cook the meals, your spouse could be responsible for washing the dishes afterward. If your children are old enough, they could have a task that they are responsible for each week, such as taking out the trash. You can keep this consistent or rotate who is responsible for a particular task each week.

- If you prefer to get everything done in one fell swoop, have a time set aside each week for cleaning together as a family. For example, set aside one or two hours each Thursday night to get all the cleaning done.

- A wise woman once said, "Don't put it down, put it away." Rather than setting items down when you get home or finish an activity, always put them away right then. It doesn't take much more time to put away a coat than to drop it on a chair, and it will keep that clutter away!

- Other great ideas:

_____

_____

_____

_____

_____

_____

_____

General Home Organization

Create a family command central for your home on a wall in your kitchen or on a desk. You can keep your grocery lists, folders for each child with homework or papers to be signed, and to-do lists in one place so you can keep all these paper items together.

Keep a laundry basket handy. When guests come over, sweep any clutter into the laundry basket for quick and easy cleanup. You can also do a quick sweep with a laundry basket every morning to pick up and put away those things that are lying around on floors or countertops.

- In an entryway or mudroom, have a hook and cubby or shelf for each member of the family. Have each child be responsible for hanging up his or her own coat and putting away shoes and other items in a cubbyhole.

- Have nice-looking boxes or bins to store miscellaneous accumulations. For example, keep a basket for all the mail, magazines, and other items that seem to always cover your dining table or desk.

- Routinely get rid of clutter. Every six months or once a year, do a sweep of the house to find items you haven't used. If you haven't used them in six months to a year, donate them to charity.

- Other great ideas:

_____

_____

_____

_____

_____

_____

Connecting With God

"Good planning and hard work lead to prosperity, but hasty shortcuts lead to poverty." (Proverbs 21:5)

- In what ways do you think good planning can lead to prosperity?

_____

_____

_____

_____

- Have you ever had an experience of this—or of the opposite?

_____

_____

_____

_____

"We can make our plans, but the Lord determines our steps." (Proverbs 16:9)

- We can make plans to get organized and get in control our lives, but ultimately God is in control. How can we balance organizing our lives, while still remembering to trust in God—because he is in control, and not us?

_____

_____

_____

_____

Connecting to My Life

Write down what you think God would like you to take away from today's session.

_____

_____

_____

_____

_____

_____

_____

_____

_____

_____

_____

_____

_____

_____

_____

_____

_____

"For I can do everything through Christ who gives me strength." (Philippians 4:13)

Additional Thoughts on Getting Organized

One reason many moms feel overwhelmed in the area of organization is that we set the bar too high. There are plenty of times when "good enough" really is good enough.

Did the laundry get washed and dried, and now everyone can find what they need in a pile in the dining room? That might be good enough for today.

Did everyone get something to eat for dinner—even if it was mac and cheese from a box? Good enough.

Choose the things that really matter, and say "good enough" to the rest. You only have your kids around for a few years, and when they're grown, you won't really care if they had their clothes ironed and hung in the closet each night or if there was toothpaste on the bathroom sink.

If you can plop down at the end of today and smile at the memory of a hug from one of your kids—that's good enough! ☺

Notes

_____

_____

_____

_____

_____

_____

_____

_____

_____

_____

_____

_____

_____

_____

_____

_____

_____

_____

_____

Keeping Secrets

Connecting to the Topic

When to Share a Secret

You were asked to keep a secret. You *swore* you'd do so. But now—you're not so sure. When should you spill a secret...no matter what you promised?

Tell a secret if...

• Someone's safety and wellbeing are in jeopardy—including the wellbeing of the person who told you the secret.

• The secret requires you lie to others and close off communication.

• The secret actively deceives others and sets them up for disappointment or pain.

• The cost of keeping the secret is simply too heavy to bear.

Note that it's important *how* and *with whom* you share someone's secret.

Tell *only* someone who has the authority and expertise to help you or the person who told you the secret. And be aware that telling—even if it's necessary—may cost you a relationship.

"For the Lord sees every heart and knows every plan and thought. If you seek him, you will find him." (1 Chronicles 28:9)

"Then you will know the truth, and the truth will set you free." (John 8:32)

Connecting to My Life

Additional Thoughts on Keeping Secrets

Psalm 139 is a beautiful reminder of how dear we are to God. He made every detail of our being, knows our every thought, and loves us, no matter what. Take time this week to read and reread these words. Circle the ones that touch your heart. Write notes about what these words mean to you. There are no secrets with God—and that's wonderful!

"O Lord, you have examined my heart and know everything about me.

You know when I sit down or stand up.

You know my thoughts even when I'm far away.

You see me when I travel and when I rest at home.

You know everything I do.

You know what I am going to say even before I say it, Lord.

You go before me and follow me.

You place your hand of blessing on my head.

Such knowledge is too wonderful for me, too great for me to understand!

I can never escape from your Spirit!

I can never get away from your presence!

If I go up to heaven, you are there; if I go down to the grave, you are there.

If I ride the wings of the morning, if I dwell by the farthest oceans, even there your hand will guide me, and your strength will support me.

I could ask the darkness to hide me and the light around me to become night—but even in darkness I cannot hide from you.

To you the night shines as bright as day.

Darkness and light are the same to you.

You made all the delicate, inner parts of my body and knit me together in my mother's womb.

Thank you for making me so wonderfully complex!

Your workmanship is marvelous—how well I know it.

You watched me as I was being formed in utter seclusion, as I was woven together in the dark of the womb.

You saw me before I was born.

Every day of my life was recorded in your book.

Every moment was laid out before a single day had passed.

How precious are your thoughts about me, O God.

They cannot be numbered!

I can't even count them; they outnumber the grains of sand!

And when I wake up, you are still with me!"

"Search me, O God, and know my heart; test me and know my anxious thoughts.

Point out anything in me that offends you, and lead me along the path of everlasting life."

(Psalm 139:1-18, 23-24)

Family Mealtimes

Connecting to the Topic

_____

_____

_____

_____

_____

_____

_____

_____

_____

_____

_____

_____

_____

_____

Connecting With God

One mom in the group can read these verses aloud:

"Children are a gift of the Lord; they are a reward from him. Children born to a young man are like arrows in a warrior's hands. How joyful is the man whose quiver is full of them!" (Psalm 127:3-5)

"A gentle answer deflects anger, but harsh words make tempers flare." (Proverbs 15:1)

"Let your conversation be gracious and attractive so that you will have the right response for everyone." (Colossians 4:6)

- What words do you use to let your children know they are a gift?

_____

_____

_____

_____

_____

- What does it mean that children are "like arrows in warrior's hands"?

_____

_____

_____

_____

_____

- How do these verses encourage you as you seek to have meaningful family mealtimes?

_____

_____

_____

_____

_____

- How could you use one or more of these verses to encourage more grace-filled conversation in your own home?

_____

_____

_____

_____

_____

Connecting to My Life

_____

_____

_____

_____

_____

Additional Thoughts on Family Mealtimes

The King James Version of Psalm 98:4 says, "Make a joyful noise unto the Lord." While some people think this means joyful singing or shouting, there are others who think the most joyful noise of all is laughter!

As you're engaging your family at mealtimes, be sure there's lots of joyful noise going on. Here are a few silly jokes you can tell to get your kids laughing (or groaning...or rolling their eyes saying "Oh mom...")

Why don't cats like to go camping?
They're afraid of the pup tents!

What's green and smells like paint?
Green paint!

Knock knock.
Who's there?
Jess.
Jess who?
I give up, who?

Check out a book of silly jokes
at the library, and see if you
can make each other laugh
the next time you're gathered
for a meal. Make a joyful noise!

Confronting Bullies

Connecting With God

Tips From the Experts

- Debrief at dinner.

- Listen.

- Practice dealing with bullies.

- Be assertive.

- Be aware of context.

- Other ideas:

Connecting to My Life

Here's a helpful website to help you understand more about bullying and how you, as a mom, can be involved in creating solutions: stopbullying.gov.

Additional Thoughts on Bullies

Bullies aren't limited to schools or workplaces. Many women avoid gatherings at church (such as moms' ministry!) because they've been bullied. This might sound odd—grown women being bullies at church? Just because we're grown doesn't mean we stop being bullies. It only means we're more subtle in how we bully. Here's what bullying might look like for adult women.

- Snobs. Women who have money or status, have been at the church a long time, have nice clothes, or literally anything else they can use to make themselves seem better or more important than others.

- Women who make "catty" comments. Spreading gossip, making mean-spirited comments, and spreading rumors are all bullying. Sadly, in church you might see this thinly veiled as "prayer requests."

- Imposters. These women will fake a friendship if it seems there's something they can get in return. When the "friendship" doesn't get them what they want, they turn on the other person. Ouch.

As moms, we're often protective of our kids and assume that someone else is the bully. Let's take a careful look at our own lives and see what we're modeling for our children.

"Then keep your tongue from speaking evil and your lips from telling lies!" (Psalm 34:13)

Encouragement

for Single or Lonely Moms

Connecting With God

Creativity

Curiosity

Critical thinking

Love of learning

Wisdom

Bravery

Persistence

Integrity

Vitality

Love

Kindness

Social intelligence

Citizenship

Fairness

Leadership

Forgiveness and mercy

Humility

Prudence

Self-control

Appreciation of beauty
and excellence

Gratitude

Hope

Humor

Faith

Circle the personal characteristics you feel are strengths for you.

- Taking turns, share with your small group the characteristics you chose and why. Ask any moms who know you well if they see additional strengths, and circle those to indicate ones other people see in you (that maybe you missed).

- Discuss how you think these individual strengths help you build a balanced and happy life.

Have one mom read the following Scripture verse:

"God arms me with strength, and he makes my way perfect." (Psalm 18:32)

- How does faith in God help strengthen us? How does faith help us find the perfect in the midst of imperfection?

_____

_____

_____

_____

_____

_____

_____

_____

_____

_____

Have another mom read these verses:

"Instead, we will speak the truth in love, growing in every way more and more like Christ, who is the head of his body, the church. He makes the whole body fit together perfectly. As each part does its own special work, it helps the other parts grow, so that the whole body is healthy and growing and full of love." (Ephesians 4:15-16)

- What is our responsibility, as parts of the body of Christ, to help each other grow and become healthy? How can we more specifically support and encourage single moms in building balanced and happy lives?

_____

_____

_____

_____

_____

_____

_____

_____

_____

_____

_____

_____

_____

Connecting to My Life

_____

_____

_____

_____

_____

_____

_____

_____

_____

_____

_____

_____

_____

_____

_____

_____

_____

Additional Thoughts
for Single or Lonely Moms

When you're feeling lonely or like you're doing momhood alone, it can be awkward to just call someone and say "I'm lonely. Can you come over?" Here are some reasons to call another mom and get together—reasons that will give you lots of opportunities to talk and encourage each other:

- Let's go for a walk!

- Will you try a new class at the gym with me?

- Let's take our kids to the park, sit on a bench, and eat ice cream while they play.

- Wanna help me paint my living room?

- We have a ping-pong table in our garage—come over, and let's see if we remember how to play!

- Let's get coffee!

- Come sit in my car with me while we wait for our kids to be released from kindergarten—I'll keep the heater on so we don't freeze!

- Bring your kids over, and they can watch a movie while we bake muffins...or just eat the ones I picked up at the bakery.

- Let's rake leaves for my elderly neighbor—the kids can help!

- As you think of other ideas you can try, jot them down here.

_____

_____

_____

_____

Notes

_____
_____
_____
_____
_____
_____
_____
_____
_____
_____
_____
_____
_____
_____
_____
_____
_____
_____

Overwhelmed by Life

Connecting to My Life

Denise's Life Lessons

- Lightning can strike anywhere—including your home.

- Neighbors make valuable friends...get to know them.

- Don't take one minute of this life for granted.

- Disaster lets you know who your true friends are, and they may not be who you thought they were.

- A toothbrush and the kind person who gave it to you can be the highlight of your day...and a reminder that there's hope after all.

- Life may kick you down, but it's your attitude that determines if you stay there.

- People, in general, are amazingly kind.

- Fear stops many people from stepping forward to help others.

- It's humbling to accept help from others.

- Give what you would want to receive.

- When you put yourself in someone else's shoes, you can walk through pain with that person...and provide a lifetime of comfort.

- Patience isn't easy...but trusting God makes it easier.

- There may always be another hard experience coming... knowing God is with you makes it bearable.

- Life isn't fair, but God's grace can make up for the imbalance.

- Bad days will pass. Really.

- Live one day at a time, even minute by minute, if necessary.

- People before things. Every time.

- Never miss the chance to show people you love that you love them. There will never be another opportunity quite like that one, ever again.

- Prayer is good therapy.

- Giving feels different from receiving. It's good to learn to do both. You'll be a better giver if you've experienced the other side of that coin.

- It's OK to cry and express your pain. A friend who will do that with you is a true friend, indeed.

- Never underestimate the power of a seemingly small gesture.

- Today's priority may not be a priority at all tomorrow. It can all change in an instant.

- Remember lessons you've learned in your past. You'll draw on them in the future.

Additional Thoughts on Feeling Overwhelmed by Life

"The Lord is my shepherd; I shall not want."
(Psalm 23:1, KJV)

Can you imagine telling a 2-year-old they "shall not want"? They *do* want! They want candy bars at the store. They want their sibling's toys. They want doughnuts for dinner. A child wants a lot of things, but a mom can say "no" if it's something the child doesn't *need.*

As grown women, we have wants, too. And sometimes our wants are not so different! (Bring on the chocolate!) But we have a heavenly Father who can say "no." Just like the 2-year-old, we don't always get what we *want,* but 2 Peter 1:3 says, "By his divine power, God has given us everything we need for living a godly life."

When life gets stressful, we may think we really *need* that chocolate bar! But the Lord knows what we *really* need. He's aware of the stresses and messes of our lives, and he knows when we're hungry, tired, or afraid. He hears our cries for help. He carries us when we are too weak to go on. He searches for us when we become hopelessly lost.

God shepherds us with love as "the sheep of his pasture" (Psalm 100:3). He knows our deepest wants *are* our needs. Life is exhausting—we need rest. Life is chaotic—we need peace. Life is lonely—we need love. Life is difficult—we need help! God answers our wants by promising us exactly what we need.

The Lord is our shepherd. We shall not want.
What is your deepest "want" today?

Psalm 23

I want someone to help me.
The Lord is my shepherd; I have all that I need.

I want rest.
He lets me rest in green meadows;

I want peace.
He leads me beside peaceful streams.

I want strength.
He renews my strength.

I want guidance.
He guides me along right paths, bringing honor to his name.

I want courage.
Even when I walk through the darkest valley, I will not be afraid, for you are close beside me.

I want to feel safe.
Your rod and your staff protect and comfort me.

I want to overcome adversity.
You prepare a feast for me in the presence of my enemies.

I want to feel valued.
You honor me by anointing my head with oil.

I want to feel blessed.
My cup overflows with blessings.

I want to be loved.
Surely your goodness and unfailing love will pursue me all the days of my life,

I want a home.
And I will live in the house of the Lord forever.

Notes

Notes

Notes

Notes

A Moms Book of Encouragement

Notes

Notes

A Mom's Book of Encouragement